Cats

Educational Poems

By

Nikki Hughey

For

Grandma and grandpa Laugherty

Abyssinian cat

Hello I'm an Abyssinian

I'm from India

I came to America in 1935

I'm very smart

I love to play, go for walks, and learn tricks

I like older children

I will tolerate other pets

I hate to be alone

I love to watch birds

I'm prone to pyruvate kinase deficiency

I need my nails trimmed every two weeks

I need brushed weekly

I need my teeth brushed daily

Acinonyx jubatus raineyii

Hello I'm a cheetah

I can live up to 14 years

I live in East Africa

I can be up to 160 pounds

I can be up to 5 feet long

I live in woodlands, savannah, and desert

Girls live alone or with babies

Boys live alone or in a group of up to 4 cheetahs

I eat gazelle, impala, kob, springbok, warthog, blackbuck,

lesser kudu, hare, and guinea fowl

Brothers spend their entire lives together

Acinonyx jubatus soemmeringii

Hello I'm a cheetah

I live in Africa

I'm vulnerable

I can run up to 87 kilometers per hour

I cannot retract my claws

I like the grass savanna

I'm protected by law

Acinonyx jubatus velox

Hello I'm a cheetah

I'm not a panther but I'm a big cat

I'm awake during the day

I can leap across 7 meters at once

Most of my muscles are made of slow twitching fibers

I can't climb trees

It takes me three seconds to reach 100 kilometers per hour

I start hunting at just 7 months old

Aegean

Hello I'm an Aegean

I like to play and hunt

I'm friendly

I can be up to 10 pounds

I can live up to 15 years

I'm from Greece

I love fish

I like water

I like children and other pets

I like to meow

I'm prone to diabetes

I need daily tooth brushing

I need weekly brushing

African golden cat

Hello I'm an African golden cat

I can be up to 40 inches long

My tail can be up to 18.1 inches long

I can be up to 35 pounds

I eat birds, antelope, monkeys, and hyraxes

I like to live alone

I start walking at 13 days old

I can live up to 12 years (captive)

African leopard

Hello I'm an African Leopard

I can live up to 12 years (wild) 23 years (captive)

I spend the first 18 months with my mom

I like to live alone

I can live almost anywhere from a rainforest to the side of

a volcano

I like to swim and climb trees

I eat boar, giraffe, beetles, zebra, baboon, and wildebeest

I'm awake at night

I take my food to the top of a tree before I eat

I eat 900 pounds of meat per year

I'm vulnerable

African wild cat

Hello I'm an African wild cat

I was domesticated 10,000 years ago

I could be up to 23.5 inches long

I could be up to 9.9 pounds

I live in Africa and the Middle East

I'm awake at night

I eat mice, rats, insects, reptiles, and birds

I live with my mom for the first 6 months

My picture is on many postage stamps

American curl

Hello I'm an American curl

I can be up to twelve pounds

I can be up to thirteen years old

I'm friendly and playful

The first American curl was born in California in 1981

I need lots of grooming

American lion

Hello I'm an American lion

I lived between Alaska and Peru

I went extinct 13,000 years ago

I ate mammoths, bison, deer, horses, and camels

My canine teeth were ten centimeters long

I could be up to 774 pounds

I could be up to 11.5 feet long

Boys did not have a mane

American wirehair

Hello I'm an American wire

hair

The first American wirehair was born in 1966 in

Vermont

We became our own breed in 1967

I'm quiet but playful

I don't need much grooming

I prefer to stay indoors

The first American wirehair was the son of an American

shorthair cat

Amur leopard

Hello I'm an Amur leopard

I can be up to forty-eight kilograms

I can live up to twenty years (captive)

I live with my mom for two years

I can run up to 35 miles per hour

I like to carry my food up a tree then eat it

I eat deer, hares, and badgers

I'm critically endangered

I live in the forest of Russia, China, and Korea

Anatolian leopard

Hello I'm an Anatolian leopard

I'm critically endangered

I'm from Turkey

I'm one of the big cats that had to fight in the colosseums

of ancient Rome

I was once believed to be extinct

I can be over 100 kilograms

The biggest threat I face is trophy hunting

Andean mountain cat

Hello I'm an Andean mountain cat

I like to live alone

I live in the Andes

I'm not afraid of people

I eat rodents

I'm very hard to study

Only 2 scientists have seen me

Aphrodite giant

Hello I'm an Aphrodite giant

I like children and other pets

I like attention

I can live up to 15 years

I'm from Cyprus

I like to be groomed

I hate being alone

I can have long or short hair

Arabian leopard

Hello I'm an Arabian leopard

I could be up to 31 inches tall

I could be up to 65 inches long

Boys could be up to 200 pounds

Girls could be up to 130 pounds

I live in the mountains near large sources of water

The biggest threats I face are habitat loss and hunting

Arabian mau

Hello I'm an Arabian mau

I can be up to 10 inches tall

I can be up to 16 pounds

I can live up to 14 years

I'm playful and friendly

I like children and other pets

I'm awake at night

I'm smart

I need nail trimming and brushing occasionally

I need daily tooth brushing

Arabian wild cat

Hello I'm an Arabian wild cat

I can be up to 18 pounds

I can be up to 16 inches tall

I can be up to 46 inches long

I live in forests, savannah, grassland, and woodland

I like rocks

I can live up to 15 years (captive)

I like to live alone

I eat rodents, hares, arachnids, amphibians, birds, reptiles, insects, and antelope

I spend the first 5 months living with my mom

Ashera

Hello I'm an Ashera

I like to climb and play

I can be up to four feet tall on my back legs

I can weigh up to thirty pounds

I like children

I like to go for walks

I like a warm place to sleep

I'm from Los Angeles

I can live up to twenty-five years

Asian semi long hair

Hello I'm an Asian semi long hair

I'm loving and playful

I'm also called a Tiffany

The first Asian semi long hair was born in the 1980s

I like children and other pets

I like to explore

I can be very vocal especially if I'm in a small space

I'm smart

I need lots of grooming

I can live up to 15 years

Asiatic cheetah

Hello I'm An Asiatic cheetah

I live in Iran

I'm critically endangered

I was once kept by people who used me like a blood

hound

I can be up to 53 inches long

I can be up to 119 pounds

I like the desert

The biggest threats I face are poaching and car accidents

My home can be up to 93 miles wild

I eat hare, sheep, and gazelle

Asiatic lion

Hello I'm an Asiatic lion

I can be up to 110 centimeters tall

I can be up to 280 centimeters long

I can be up to 190 kilograms

I'm endangered

Habitat loss has forced me to hunt farm animals

I'm from India

Australian mist

Hello I'm an Australian mist

Before 1998 I was called a spotted mist

I'm playful and loving

I'm smart

I like to be indoors

I like children

I can live up to 13 years

The first Australian mist was born in 1976

I like other pets

I tolerate being held and I like to sit on your lap

Balearic wild cat

Hello I'm a Balearic wild cat

I'm from Spain

I eat rodents, birds, and reptiles

I can be up to 46 inches long

I can be up to 18 pounds

I can run up to 30 miles per hour

I like to live alone

I'm awake at night

I can live up to 8 years (wild) 15 years (captive)

I spend the first 5 months with my mom

Bali tiger

Hello I'm a Bali tiger

I went extinct in 1930

I could be up to 6.5 feet long

I could be up to 220 pounds

I ate boar, pig, bird, monitor lizard, deer, antelope, and

buffalo

My home was ten square miles long

I liked to live alone

I was hunted for my fur and teeth

I lost my habitat to farm land

Balinese cat

Hello I'm a Balinese

The first Balinese was born before 1871

We became our own breed in 1979

I like kids and other pets

I love playing, walking, and learning tricks

I like to talk

I'm very smart

I'm prone to lysosomal storage disease and feline

acromelanism

I need weekly brushing and nail trimming

I need daily tooth brushing

Bambino

Hello I'm a Bambino

I can be up to 8 inches tall

I can be up to 9 pounds

I can be up to 15 years old

I'm loving and playful

I like children and other pets

The first Bambino was born in 2005

I like to cuddle

I need regular baths

Barbary lion

Hello I'm a Barbary lion

I went extinct in the mid twentieth
century

I lived in forest and mountain tops

I lived in Africa

I could be up to nine feet long

I could be up to 300 kilograms

I ate antelope, pigs, boar, deer, and buffalo

I could live up to fifteen years

I was very popular in circuses and zoos

I went extinct due to hunting and deforestation

I was just 13 days old when I learned to walk

Bay cat

Hello I'm a Bay cat

I can be up to 10 pounds

I live in Borneo

I live in the forest

I like limestone and rivers

My habitat is threatened by logging

Bengal

Hello I'm a Bengal

I can be up to twelve pounds

I'm very smart

I love to explore, play, and climb

I will get into your fish tank or shower

I can be up to sixteen years old

I'm prone to patella, retinal, and hip problems

I'm prone to hypertrophic cardiomyopathy

I'm a mix of a domestic cat and a wild cat

I'm considered domestic

The first Bengal was born in 1963

Bengal tiger

Hello I'm a Bengal tiger

I'm from India

I have 4-inch-long canine teeth

I live in forests and mangrove swamps

I eat buffalo, deer, and boar

I can eat up to 40 kilograms in one meal

I like to live alone but I live with my mom for the first 3

years

Birman

Hello I'm a Birman

I'm from France

The first Birman was born in 1919

I like children and other pets

I'm loving and playful

I can live up to fifteen years

I need to be brushed every week

I need my nails trimmed every two weeks

Black footed cat

Hello I'm a black footed cat

I can live up to 13 years (captive)

I can be up to 17 inches long

I can be up to 10 inches tall

I can be up to 4.2 pounds

I live in Africa

My home is up to 8.5 square miles

I'm awake at night

I like to live alone

I live with my mom for the first five months

I eat small mammals, birds, insects, arachnids, and

reptiles

I'm vulnerable

Black panther

Hello I'm a black panther

I'm most likely a jaguar or a leopard

I have melanism which makes my fur all black

I can produce both black cubs and cubs who don't have

melanism

I'm more easily startled than cats without melanism

Bob cat

Hello I'm a bob cat

I live in the United States and Canada

I can be up to 30 pounds

I can be up to 50 inches long

I live in forest, deserts, and swamps

I'm hunted for my fur

Hunting me became illegal in 1970

I can live up to 13 years (wild) 20 years (captive)

I like to live alone

I eat rabbit, rodents, deer, birds, bats, beaver, and

peccaries

Bombay cat

Hello I'm a Bombay cat

I can be up to eleven pounds

I like to play and learn tricks

I like children and other pets

I'm prone to a craniofacial defect

I can be up to sixteen years old

The first Bombay was born in the 1950s

Brazilian shorthair

Hello I'm a Brazilian shorthair

It is believed though unlikely that the first Brazilian

shorthair was born in 1500

I'm loving and affectionate

I like children and other pets

I'm smart

I can be up to 15 years old

I can be up to 12 pounds

British long hair

Hello I'm a British long hair

I'm friendly and independent

I like children and other pets

I can be up to 17 years old

I can be up to 14 inches tall

I can be up to 18 pounds

The first British long hair was born in 1918

I'm quite

I'm prone to being overweight

I'm not as playful as other cats

I need to be brushed at least once a week

British semi long hair

Hello I'm a British semi long hair

I come from the 19th century

I'm a mix of the Persian and the British short hair

I'm prone to kidney trouble

British shorthair

Hello I'm a British shorthair

The Roman army brought me to Britain so I could

protect their food supply from rodents

I like children and other pets

I enjoy playing but I'm very chill

I'm loving and smart

I'm prone to hemophilia b and hypertrophic

cardiomyopathy

I need weekly nail trimming and brushing

I need daily tooth brushing

Burmese cat

Hello I'm a Burmese

The first Burmese was born in the 1920s

We became our own breed in 1957

I like children and other pets

I like to learn tricks and solve puzzles

I like to talk and cuddle

I'm prone to stones in the urinary track, cranial

deformities, glaucoma, and feline hyperaesthesia

I need daily tooth brushing

I need weekly nail trimming and brushing

Burmilla

Hello I'm a Burmilla

The first Burmilla was born in 1981

I'm playful and smart

I like to explore

I like children and other pets

I'm prone to allergies and kidney disease

I need daily tooth brushing

I need weekly combing and nail trimming

California spangled

Hello I'm a California spangled

I'm friendly and playful

I like children and other pets

I can be up to 10 inches tall

I can be up to 15 pounds

I can be up to 16 years old

The first California spangled was born in 1985

I like to climb

I hate to be alone

I'm very smart

I need a weekly brushing

I enjoy being groomed

Canadian lynx

Hello I'm a Canadian lynx

I live in forests

I live in Alaska and Canada

I can live up to 15 years (wild) 21 years (captive)

I may spend months with my siblings after we leave mom

but I like to live alone

I eat snowshoe hare

I'm threatened

The biggest threats I face are habitat loss and hunting

cape lion

Hello I'm a cape lion

I went extinct 100 years ago due to habitat loss and

hunting

I could be up to 7 feet long

I could be up to 500 pounds

I could be up to 10 years old

I ate deer, antelope, zebra, buffalo, and giraffe

The last cape lion died in 1876 at the age of two

Caracal

Hello I'm a caracal

I was once used by bird hunters

I can be up to 40 pounds

I can be up to 39 inches long

I live in forest, savannah, and woodlands

I live in Asia, Africa, and the Middle East

I'm threatened by getting hunted for eating farm animals

I eat rodents, hares, antelope, and hyraxes

I can live up to 19 years (captive)

I spend the first year with my mom

I like to live alone

I'm awake at night

Caraval

Hello I'm a caraval

My mom was a serval

My dad was a caracal

The first caraval was born at the Los Angeles zoo

I'm considered a pet

I only exist in captivity

Cashmere cat

Hello I'm a cashmere cat

I'm playful and friendly

I like children and other pets

I can be up to 10 inches tall

I can be up to 15 pounds

I can be up to 15 years old

The first Cashmere cat was born in the 1980s

Its parents were Bengals

We became our own breed in 2017

I need the same grooming as a Bengal

I like to climb

I like to talk

I like water

Caspian tiger

Hello I'm a Caspian tiger

I could be up to 500 pounds

I ate pigs

I lost my habitat to farm land

The last Caspian tiger died in 1970

Hunting me became illegal in 1953

Caucasian wild cat

Hello I'm a Caucasian wild cat

I live in Turkey

I live in the mountains

I can be up to 18 pounds

I can be up to 11 inches tall

I can be up to 30 inches long

I was first discovered in 1916

Chantilly

Hello I'm a Chantilly

I need daily brushing

I can be up to 12 pounds

I can be up to 12 years old

I'm friendly and playful

I'm prone to being overweight

The first Chantilly was born in New York in 1969

Chartreux

Hello I'm a Chartreux

I'm from France

The first Chartreux was born before the 18th century

I'm quiet

I'm playful and intelligent

I like to sit on your lap

I like children and other pets

I'm prone to stones in the urinary track and kidney

disease

I need my teeth brushed daily

I need to be combed weekly

I need my nails trimmed weekly

Chausie

Hello I'm a Chausie

I like other pets and older children

I'm friendly and playful

I can be up to 14 years old

I can be up to 30 pounds

I can be up to 18 inches tall

The first Chausie was born in 1990

I'm very smart

Never feed me any plants as I can't digest them

I can jump up to 8 feet high

I need to be brushed weekly

Cheetah

Hello I'm a cheetah

I can run up to 70 miles per hour

People started keeping me captive 5000 years ago

I can be up to 145 pounds

I can be up to 86 inches long

I live in grasslands, savannas, and mountains

I'm endangered

I have a weak immune system

I live with my mom for the first two years

Girls live alone but boys stay with their brothers for life

I eat gazelle and some other animals

I can live 10 days without water

Cheetoh

Hello I'm a Cheetoh

I'm smart and friendly

I'm playful

I like children and other pets

I can be up to 14 years old

I can be up to 14 inches tall

I can be up to 23 pounds

The first cheetoh was born in 2001

Its parents were a Bengal and an Ocicat

I like to talk and cuddle

I need weekly brushing

Chinese mountain cat

Hello I'm a Chinese mountain cat

I live in Tibet

I can be up to 20 pounds

I can be up to 47 inches long

I like to live alone

I'm awake at night

I eat rodents

The biggest threat I face is rat poison

I live with my mom for the first eight months

clouded leopard

Hello I'm a clouded leopard

I can't roar or purr

I like to swim and climb trees

I can be up to 45 pounds

I can live up to 11 years (wild) 17 years (captive)

I like mangrove swamps, forests, and grasslands

I live between Nepal and Borneo

I eat deer, birds, small mammals, boar, porcupines, and primates

I'm vulnerable

color point shorthair

Hello I'm a color point shorthair

I can be up to twelve pounds

I can be up to twelve years old

I'm very smart

I love to play

I love to jump and climb

I enjoy being groomed

Congo lion

Hello I'm a Congo lion

I like to climb trees

I like to swim

I have lived in the Congo for the past 120,000 years

It is not likely that I originated in the Congo

I'm not seen often

People thought I was extinct for 20 years

Cornish rex

Hello I'm a Cornish rex

The first Cornish rex was born in 1950

I'm energetic, smart, and loveable

I like dogs and kids

I like to travel and learn tricks

I love to play

I'm prone to knee trouble and heart disease

I need weekly nail trimming and tooth brushing

Corsican wild cat

Hello I'm a Corsican wild cat

I'm like a fox

I'm a close relative of the African wild cat

The Roman army brought me to Corsica in 6000 BC

Cougar

Hello I'm a cougar

I can be up to 9 feet long

I can be up to 150 pounds

I live in North and South America

I like to live alone

I live with my mom for the first two years

I can live up to 10 years (wild) 20 years (captive)

Cymric

Hello I'm a Cymric

I have no tail

I'm from the Isle of Man

I like to talk, play, and climb

I like to learn tricks

I'm smart

I like children and other pets

I may have a spinal defect

I need daily tooth brushing

I need weekly nail trimming

I need to be brushed 3 times a week

Cyprus

Hello I'm a Cyprus

I'm one of the world's oldest cat breeds

I'm 4000 years older than the Egyptian mau

Most of us are feral

I'm energetic and I love to play

I like children and other pets

I can be up to 12 pounds

I can be up to 15 years old

Devon rex

Hello I'm a Devon rex

I'm very smart and friendly

I like other pets

I love to play

I should be kept indoors

I like older children

I like to learn tricks

Domestic medium hair

Hello I'm a domestic medium hair

I'm a mutt

I'm energetic and playful

I like children and other pets

I can be up to 17 years old

I can be up to 22 pounds

I can be up to 14 inches tall

I need brushed weekly

I'm not very different from the domestic long hair

Domestic short hair

Hello I'm a domestic short hair

I can be up to 15 pounds

I can be up to 20 years old

I'm a mutt

I'm loving and playful

I like children and other pets

I'm prone to obesity

I'm active at night

I need daily tooth brushing

I need weekly nail trimming and brushing

Donskoy

Hello I'm a Donskoy

I'm from Russia

I'm very social and smart

I need weekly baths

I have webbed toes

I can be up to seven kilograms

The first Donskoy was born in 1987

I love to meow

Dragon li

Hello I'm a dragon li

I'm Chinese

I'm a good hunter

I'm smart, friendly, and playful

I like children and other pets

Keep me indoors as I am very rare

I can be up to 12 pounds

I can be up to 15 years old

Dwelf

Hello I'm a dwelf

I can be up to 7 inches tall

I can be up to 9 pounds

I can be up to 15 years old

I'm friendly, playful, and smart

I like children and other pets

I may have skeletal problems

I hate to be alone

I need a weekly bath

I have no fur so keep me indoors

East African lion

Hello I'm an East African lion

I can be up to 3.3 meters long

I can be up to 250 kilograms

I can be up to 15 years old (wild) 30 years old (captive)

I like grasslands

I eat giraffe, buffalo, deer, and carrion

East African wild cat

Hello I'm an East African wild cat

I can be up to 75 centimeters long

I can be up to 6.5 kilograms

I live in brushland, savannah, and steppes

I eat birds, reptiles, insects, rats, mice, and amphibians

I'm awake at night

I like to live alone

I can live up to 15 years

I spend the first 6 months with my mom

Egyptian mau

Hello I'm an Egyptian mau

I was worshipped in ancient Egypt

I'm very athletic and smart

I love my people but I'm shy around others

I'm prone to leuodystrophy

I need regular tooth brushing

I need weekly nail trimming and brushing

Elf cat

Hello I'm an elf cat

The first elf cat was born in 2007

I need two baths per week

I have no fur so keep me indoors

I can be up to 15 pounds

I'm loving and playful

Eurasian cave lion

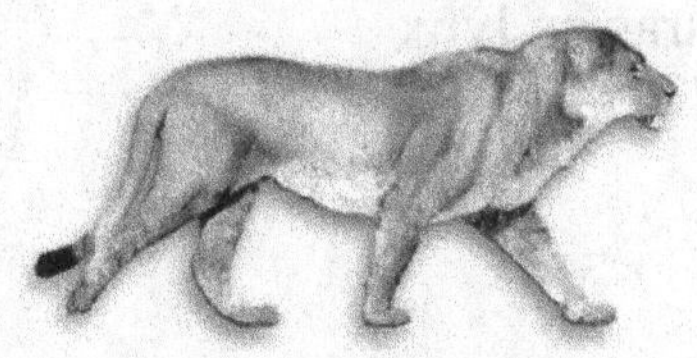

Hello I'm a Eurasian cave

lion

I went extinct 12,000 years ago

I could be up to seven feet long

I could be up to eight hundred pounds

I eat horses, bears, and elephants

I lived in Eurasia, Alaska, and Canada

Multiple cave lions have been found in Russia

Eurasian lynx

Hello I'm a Eurasian lynx

I like to live alone

I was once hunted for my fur

I'm endangered

I can be up to 130 centimeters long

I can be up to 40 kilograms

I like rocks and trees

I'm awake at dawn and dusk

I eat deer, birds, and sheep

I can live up to 20 years (captive) 13 years (wild)

European Burmese cat

Hello I'm a European Burmese

cat

I can be up to twelve inches tall

I can be up to fourteen pounds

I can be up to fifteen years old

The first European Burmese was born in 1930

I do not need much grooming but I enjoy being groomed

I'm very loving and friendly

I like children and other pets

I like to climb and play

I should be kept indoors as I will go anywhere with

anyone

European lion

Hello I'm a European lion

I went extinct 1,000 years ago

I could be up to four feet long

I could be up to 400 pounds

I was first seen by a person in the 5th century BCE

The ancient Romans used me to kill gladiators and

Christians in the 1st and 2nd centuries AD

I was hunted to extinction

European short hair

Hello I'm a European short hair

I can be up to 20 years old

I can be up to 15 pounds

I love to play

I like children and other pets

I love the outdoors

I'm shy around strangers

I need weekly nail trimming and brushing

I need daily tooth brushing

I'm from Sweden

European wild cat

Hello I'm a European wild cat

I'm from 478000 years ago

I can be up to 36 inches long

My tail can be up to 15.7 inches long

I live in the forest

I like to live alone

I'm awake at night

I don't like to climb trees

I live in the burrows that other animals abandon

I eat rabbit, rodents, and birds

I can live up to 21 years

I used to be an ingredient in various medicines

Exotic shorthair

Hello I'm an Exotic shorthair

I can live fourteen years

The first Exotic shorthair was born in the United States

I'm loveable and lazy

I need weekly grooming

The first Exotic shorthair was born in the early 1960s

We became our own breed in 1966

I like to follow my human like a shadow

I often have eye infections

I'm likely to get kidney disease

My teeth need daily brushing

Seniors need to see the vet twice a year

Fishing cat

Hello I'm a fishing cat

I can be up to 26 pounds

I can be up to 16 inches tall

I can be up to 47 inches long

I like, creeks, swamps, lakes and marshes

I eat fish

I'm good at swimming and diving

I live in India and Indonesia

I can live up to 12 years (captive)

I live with my mom for the first 10 months

The biggest threat I face is habitat loss

Flat headed cat

Hello I'm a flat headed cat

I use water and my two front paws to wash things

I can be up to 6 pounds

I like swamps

I eat fish, frog, and shrimp

I can live up to 14 years (captive)

Water pollution is the biggest threat to my habitat

I have webbed feet

Florida Panther

Hello I'm a Florida Panther

I'm a subspecies of Puma

I'm endangered

I can be up to 160 pounds

As a baby I have spots

I like swamps, forest, and grasslands

I eat armadillo, rabbit, hog, and deer

Girls and kittens stay in Florida

Boys can go as far as Georgia

I try to stay away from people but I've lost a lot of habitat

Foldex

Hello I'm a foldex

I'm from Canada

The first foldex was born in the 1990s

I'm playful and friendly

I'm curious and smart

I like children and other pets

I can be up to 15 years old

I can be up to 14 pounds

I can be up to 12 inches tall

I love to be petted

I need weekly brushing and nail trimming

Geoffroy's cat

Hello I'm a Geoffroy's cat

I love to swim

I can be up to 10 pounds

I live in the forests of South America

I can live up to 20 years (captive)

I like to live alone

I'm awake at night

I eat fish, bird, rodent, reptile, and hare

German rex

Hello I'm a German rex

I can be up to 8 pounds

I can be up to 14 years old

I'm affectionate and playful

The first German rex was born in the 1950s

Hausa wild cat

Hello I'm a Hausa wild cat

I live in Africa, the Middle East, and India

I can be up to 18 pounds

I can be up to 16 inches tall

I can be up to 46 inches long

I can live up to 15 years (captive)

I live with my mom for the first 5 months

I like to live alone

I'm awake at night

I eat hare, rodent, insect, bird, arachnid, reptile,

amphibian, and antelope

Havana brown

Hello I'm a Havana brown

I'm smart and friendly

I like children and other pets

I like to play

The first Havana brown was born in the 1950s

I'm prone to developing calcium stones in my urinary

track

I need daily tooth brushing

I need weekly brushing and nail trimming

Highlander

Hello I'm a highlander

I can be up to fifteen years old

I can be up to twenty pounds

I can be up to sixteen inches tall

The first highlander was born in 2004

I love people

I love to play

I'm very smart

I like water

I'm polydactyl

I need occasional brushing to prevent fur balls

Himalayan cat

Hello I'm a Himalayan cat

The first Himalayan cat was born in 1931 in America

I can be up to 12 pounds

I like quite

I do not like change

I don't like to climb

I should be kept indoors

I need daily brushing

I'm prone to ocular and raspatory problems

I'm prone to kidney disease

I can live up to 15 years

Iberian lynx

Hello I'm an Iberian lynx

I can be up to sixty centimeters tall

I can be up to ten kilograms

I eat deer, rabbit, rodent, sheep, birds, and boar

I'm awake at night during the summer

I live in my mom's home for twenty months

I can live up to thirteen years (Wild)

I'm critically endangered

Indian leopard

Hello I'm an Indian leopard

I'm vulnerable due to poaching and habitat loss

I can be up to 4 feet 2 inches long

I can be up to 170 pounds

I live in the forest

I live between India and Pakistan

I like to climb and swim

I'm awake at night

I can run up to 36 miles per hour

I can jump up to 9.8 feet high

I can live up to 17 years

I spend the first two with my mom

I eat deer, and tahr

Indochinese leopard

Hello I'm an Indochinese leopard

I live in the forest

I eat lesser mouse deer, boar, and macaque

I'm threatened by habitat loss, illegal hunting, and car

accidents

Indochinese tiger

Hello I'm an Indochinese tiger

I can be up to 440 pounds

I can be up to 95 inches long

I like the forest

I eat deer, boar, badger, porcupine, and monkey

I'm shy and I like to live alone

I live with my mom for up to 28 months

I'm endangered

I've lost prey and habitat to hunters and farmers

I'm hunted for my fur and because I eat farm animals

Iraqi wild cat

Hello I'm an Iraqi wild cat

I can be up to 8 kilograms

I can be up to 20 centimeters tall

I can be up to 91 centimeters long

I can live up to 15 years

I like grasslands and savannas

I live in burrows that other animals abandon

I'm awake at night

I eat birds and rodents

I spend the first 5 months with my mom

I like to live alone

Iriomote cat

Hello I'm an Iriomote cat

I can be up to 10 pounds

I can be up to 35 inches long

I live on Iriomote island which is near Japan

I live in the forest

I like to live alone

The biggest threat I face is the feral domestic cat

I'm awake at night

I can live up to 10 years (captive)

I eat fish, crab, insects, flying fox, bird, rat, amphibians,

and skinks

I'm endangered

Jagleop

Hello I'm a jagleop

My dad was a jaguar

My mom was a leopard

The first jagleop was born in 1900

It was born at the zoo in Indianapolis

It was born to bring publicity to the zoo

Jaglion

Hello I'm a Jaglion

My mom was a lion

My dad was a jaguar

Jaguar

Hello I'm a jaguar

I'm threatened by habitat and food loss

I'm threatened by illegal hunting

I can be up to 6 feet long

I can be up to 348 pounds

I can live up to 15 years

I live in South America

Jaguarundi

Hello I'm a jaguarundi

I live in central and south America

I can be up to 20 pounds

I can be up to 55 inches long

I like swamps and forests

I can live up to 15 years

I have spots as a baby

I either live alone or in a pairing

I eat fish, rodent, bird, rabbit, armadillo, frog, reptile, and

opossum

Jagulep

Hello I'm a jagulep

My mom was a leopard

My dad was a jaguar

Girls can have babies but boys can not

Jaguon

Hello I'm a jaguon

My mom was a lion

My dad was a jaguar

I only exist in captivity

Jagupard

Hello I'm a jagupard

I was born at the Chicago zoo

My dad was a jaguar

My mom was a leopard

Japanese bobtail

Hello I'm a Japanese bobtail

I love attention

I can be up to thirteen years old

I can be up to twelve pounds

I love to play

I can learn my name

I'm very smart

I love to jump and climb

The first Japanese bobtail was born in the 6th century

AD

We are considered lucky and were loved by all social

classes

Javan leopard

Hello I'm a Javan leopard

I'm critically endangered

I eat gibbon, lutung, barking deer, mouse deer, macaque,

and boar

I'm active in the early morning and late afternoon

I'm threatened by food and habitat loss

I'm threatened by poaching

I'm from 800,000 years ago

Javan tiger

Hello I'm a Javan tiger

I could be up to 311 pounds

I could be up to 98 inches tall

The last Javan tiger died in 1976

I liked forest and mountains

I ate deer, boar, birds, and reptiles

I lost my habitat to farming

Many of us lived in various zoos but we were put down

during World War 2

My favorite prey went extinct due to disease in the 1960s

Javanese

Hello I'm a Javanese

I can live up to 12 years

I can be up to 12 pounds

I'm friendly and playful

I like to jump, climb, and talk

I'm from the United States

I must have a cat tree

jungle cat

Hello I'm a jungle cat

I have been found mummified

I can weigh up to 28 pounds

I can be up to 16 inches tall and 48 inches long

As a baby I have stripes

I live between Egypt and India

I like swamps, plains, woodlands, and grasslands

I can live up to 17 years (captive)

I live in a family group like people do

Father jungle cats are extremely protective of their babies

I eat fish, rodents, birds, pigs, hares, insects, and

amphibians

Kalahari wild cat

Hello I'm a Kalahari wild cat

I can be up to 26.2 inches long

I can be up to 12.1 pounds

I'm awake at night

I like to live alone

I eat rodents, insects, birds, hare, reptiles, and amphibians

Khao Manee

Hello I'm a Khao Manee

I'm from Thailand

My name means white gem

The first Khao Manee was born before 1350

Until recently only royalty could keep me as a pet

I came to America in 1999

I'm intelligent and playful

I love to meet new people

I need weekly brushing

I'm prone to cancer

keeping me indoors is recommended

kodkod

Hello I'm a kodkod

I'm vulnerable

I can be up to 20 inches long

I can be up to 5.5 pounds

I love to climb trees

I eat birds, lizards, and rodents

I like to live alone

I can live up to 11 years (captive)

Korat

Hello I'm a Korat

I'm from Thailand

I'm considered good luck

The first Korat was born before 1350

I'm energetic, playful, and smart

I hate to be alone

I prefer to be with other Korats

I'm prone to a fatal genetic condition called

gangliosidosis

I need regular nail trimming and tooth brushing

I need brushed twice a week

Korean bobtail

Hello I'm a Korean bobtail

I can be up to 2 feet long

I can be up to 15 pounds

I can be up to 15 years old

I'm intelligent and inquisitive

I like to talk

I love attention

I need weekly brushing

I need a bath every 3 weeks

I need my nails trimmed monthly

I should be kept indoors

Korn ja

Hello I'm a Korn ja

I'm from Thailand

I'm smart and loving

I can live up to 16 years

I may or may not have fur

I can be up to 11 pounds

I'm energetic and playful

I like children and other pets

I need weekly brushing if I have fur

I need a monthly bath (no fur)

Kurilian bobtail

Hello I'm a Kurilian bobtail

I'm energetic and playful

I love everybody

I'm Russian

I'm smart

I like to learn tricks

If I'm outside I will hunt a bird

I need a daily tooth brushing

I need a weekly brushing and nail trimming

LaPerm

Hello I'm a LaPerm

The first LaPerm was born in Oregon in 1982

I like children and other pets

I love to climb and play

I'm very smart

I need regular tooth brushing and nail trimming

I need weekly brushing

leopard

Hello I'm a leopard

I'm vulnerable

I can be up to 143 ponds

I can be up to 7.5 feet long

I can be up to 2.5 feet tall

I can live up to 12 years (wild) 23 years (captive)

I like mountains, grasslands, deserts, and forest

I live in Africa

I eat carrion, fish, mammals, birds, and reptiles

I like to climb trees

I will carry my food to the top of a tree before eating it

I like to live alone

I'm awake at night unless I have young cubs

leopard cat

Hello I'm a leopard cat

I live in Asia

I don't like snow

I like woodlands and forest

I can be up to 15 pounds

I can be up to 38 inches long

As a baby I will gain 11 grams a day

I'm awake at night

I eat rodents, hare, birds, reptiles, insects, fish, and eel

I'm threatened by deforestation

I can live up to 15 years (captive) 10 years (wild)

leopon

Hello I'm a leopon

My mom is a lion

My dad is a leopard

I only exist in captivity

I can live up to 23 years

The first leopon was born in 1959

Unlike my mom I like to swim and climb trees

Liard

Hello I'm a Liard

 I'm also called a lipard

My dad was a lion

 my mom was a leopard

The first Liard was born in 1951

Liger

Hello I'm a liger

My mom is a tiger

My dad is a lion

The first liger was born in 1798

I can be up to 11.8 feet long

I can be up to 750 pounds

I can be up to 24 years old

Females can have babies but males can not

I only exist in captivity

lijagulep

Hello I'm a lijagulep

My dad was a lion

My mom was a jagulep

The first lijagulep was born in London in 1908

I only exist in captivity

li-liger

Hello I'm a li-liger

My dad was a lion

My mom was a liger

The first li-liger was born in 1943

I only exist in captivity

lion

Hello I'm a lion

I live in Africa

I eat rodents, hares, large insects, zebra, and antelope

The girls do the hunting

My pride consists of up to 12 girls, up to 6 boys, and

babies

We steal food from hyenas and cheetahs

My mother takes care of me for the first 2 years

I can also rely on all my aunts and my dad

Girls never leave the pride they were born in

I can be up to 530 pounds

I can live up to 14 years

li-tigon

Hello I'm a li-tigon

My mom was a tigon

My dad was a lion

I can be up to 11 feet long

I can be up to 798 pounds

I only exist in captivity

Lykoi

Hello I'm a Lykoi

I'm from Virginia

I was found in 2010

The Lykoi became its own breed in 2014

I'm intelligent and playful

I like to hunt in a pack

I need lots of love

I can live up to twenty years

If I'm molting, I need daily brushing

I need my nails cared for weekly

I need help keeping my eyes clean

Only bath me when it is absolutely necessary

Keep me indoors

Lynx

Hello I'm a lynx

I can be up to 40 inches long

I'm threatened

I can see a mouse 250 feet away

I eat mice, deer, hare, birds, and squirrel

I like to live alone

I'm awake at night

I like to talk

I spend my first two years with my mom

I can live up to 14.5 years (wild) 25 years (captive)

Maine coon

Hello I'm a Main coon

The first Main coon was born before 1861

I can be up to eighteen pounds

I like children and other pets

I'm a happy lap cat but I also like to play

I will follow people around

I'm prone to hip problems

I'm prone to hypertrophic cardiomyopathy and spinal

muscular atrophy

I need daily tooth brushing

I need weekly brushing

I need my nails trimmed every two weeks

Malayan

Hello I'm a Malayan cat

The first Malayan was born in Britain in 1981

I can be up to 13 pounds

I'm playful

I like children but I do not like loud noises

I like to explore

I like to cuddle

I need weekly brushing

I can live up to 18 years

Malayan tiger

Hello I'm a Malayan tiger

I can be up to 102 inches long

I can be up to 284 ponds

I like tropical forest

I eat pig, deer, goat, tapir, monkey, bear, elephant, and rhino

I'm willing to hunt in a group but I like to live alone

I've lost habitat to logging and farming

I've been hunted by farmers and for medicine

I'm endangered

I live with my mom for the first 18 months

Manx cat

Hello I'm a Manx cat

I can be up to thirteen pounds

I like people, playing, hunting, and travel

I can be up to fourteen years old

I need regular brushing

I'm prone to arthritis

I'm prone to short spine problems

I'm prone to bowl, digestive, and urinary track problems

The first Manx was born in 1750

Marbled cat

Hello I'm a marbled cat

I'm vulnerable

I live in Asia

I live in the forests

I'm awake at night

I live in the trees

I can be up to 11 pounds

I can be up to 24 inches long

I eat squirrels, rodents, birds, and bats

I like to live alone

I climbed my first tree at two months old

I can live up to 12 years (captive)

Margay

Hello I'm a Margay

I can rotate my hind legs 180 degrees

I can be up to 20 pounds

I can be up to 52 inches long

I live in South America

I like forests

I can live up to 20 years (Captive)

I eat fruit, rodents, sloth, birds, and capuchins

I'm hunted for my fur

Mekong bobtail

Hello I'm a Mekong bobtail

I can be up to 9 inches tall

I can be up to 10 pounds

I can be up to 18 years old

I'm smart, friendly, and playful

I like children and other pets

I'm from Southeast Asia

I like to climb and jump

I need occasional brushing

Mexican hairless cat

Hello I'm a Mexican hairless cat

The first Mexican hairless cat was born in 1902

It was supposedly an ancient breed

I like to cuddle and play

I like baths

I like dogs

I can be up to ten pounds

We went extinct in 1908

Mid belt wild cat

Hello I'm a mid-belt wild cat

I'm Scottish

I used to live in England and Wales too but I went extinct
there due to deforestation and hunting

I'm vulnerable and protected by law

There are less than 400 of us left

I'm from the Holocene

I'm awake at night

I try to avoid people but I'm attracted to domestic cats

I spend the first 5 months with my mom

Minskin

Hello I'm a minskin

I can be up to fourteen years old

I can be up to six pounds

I can be up to eight inches tall

I'm friendly, playful, and intelligent

I'm from Boston

The first minskin was born in 2000

I need regular baths

I need sun block or a sweater

I like other animals and children

Mongolian wild cat

Hello I'm a Mongolian wild cat

I was discovered in 1776

I like rocks

I like to live alone

I have a wool like undercoat

I sound like a small dog

Munchkin cat

Hello I'm a Munchkin cat

The first munchkin was born in 1944

We became our own breed in 2003

I like to learn tricks

I'm very smart

I love to play

I like children and other pets

I need weekly brushing and nail trimming

I need daily tooth brushing

Napoleon

Hello I'm a Napoleon

I'm energetic and playful

I like children and other pets

I'm friendly

I can be up to 9 ponds

I can be up to 8 inches tall

I can be up to 15 years old

The first Napoleon was born in 2001

I like to cuddle

I need brushing at least once a week

Nebelung

Hello I'm a nebelung

I'm smart and loving

I'm alright with kids and other pets

I can be up to 15 pounds

I can be up to 18 years old

I'm from the United States

The first nebelung was born in 1987

I can be shy but I like to play, jump, and climb

I like a stable, quiet, affectionate home

I need daily tooth brushing

I need weekly brushing

I need my nails trimmed every two weeks

North Chinese leopard

Hello I'm a north Chinese leopard

At up to 192 centimeters long I'm the smallest big cat

I can be up to 76 kilograms

I can survive almost anywhere

I'll eat anything I can catch

I'm endangered

North west African cheetah

Hello I'm a north west African cheetah

I'm critically endangered

I was discovered in 1943

I eat gazelle

I drink blood as I don't have all the water, I need

I like to live alone

I can survive a temperature of up to 113 degrees F

Norwegian forest cat

Hello I'm a Norwegian forest cat

I'm friendly and smart

The first Norwegian forest cat was born 4000 years ago

I came to America in 1979

I like to learn tricks

I love puzzles

I tend to have hip problems

I need weekly nail trimming and hair brushing

I need daily tooth brushing

Ocelot

Hello I'm an ocelot

I like the tropics and rain

I can live up to 20 years (captive) 10 years (wild)

I'm 20 inches tall and 35 inches long

I can be up to 35 pounds

I like to live alone

I'm awake at night

I eat rats, mice, crabs, fish, tortoise, squirrel monkey,

possum, anteater, and armadillo

The biggest threat I face is habitat loss

Ocicat

Hello I'm an Ocicat

The first Ocicat was born in 1964

I'm very smart

I like to learn tricks

I like children and other pets, and even strangers

I love to climb and play

I'm prone to periodontal disease, hypertrophic

cardiomyopathy, pyruvate kinase deficiency, and liver

amyloidosis, and retinal amyloidosis

I need weekly brushing and nail trimming

I need daily tooth brushing

Ojos azules

Hello I'm an ojos azules

I like children and other pets

I'm playful and loving

I can be up to 10 inches tall

I can be up to 12 pounds

I can be up to 12 years old

I have beautiful blue eyes

The first ojos azules was born in New Mexico in 1984

I like to cuddle

I might have a bad mutation if both my parents have blue
eyes

I need regular nail trimming and brushing

Oncilla

Hello I'm an oncilla

I live in the Americas

I can be up to 21.7 inches long

I can be up to 6.6 pounds

I like to climb trees and swim

I like to live alone

I eat small mammals, eggs, birds, lizards, and

invertebrates

I open my eyes at 17 days old

I get teeth at 21 days old

I eat meat at 56 days old

I can live up to 11 years (wild) 17 years (captive)

Oregon rex

Hello I'm an Oregon rex

I went extinct in 1972

I was playful and loving

I hated to be alone

I was stubborn

I could be up to 10 pounds

I could be up to 15 years old

Oriental bicolor

Hello I'm an Oriental bicolor

I'm loving, smart, and playful

I like children and other pets

I can be up to 12 years old

I can be up to 12 pounds

I can be up to 10 inches tall

The first Oriental bicolor was born in 1979

I'm from the United States

I'm curious and talkative

I need a weekly brushing

Oriental longhair

Hello I'm an Oriental long hair

I can be up to 12 pounds

I can be up to 15 years old

I'm energetic and playful

I'm very smart

I like children and other pets

I like to cuddle and talk

I'm very curious

I need a weekly brushing

I'm prone to retinal atrophy, crossed eyes, and kidney

amyloidosis

I may have a kinked tail

Oriental shorthair

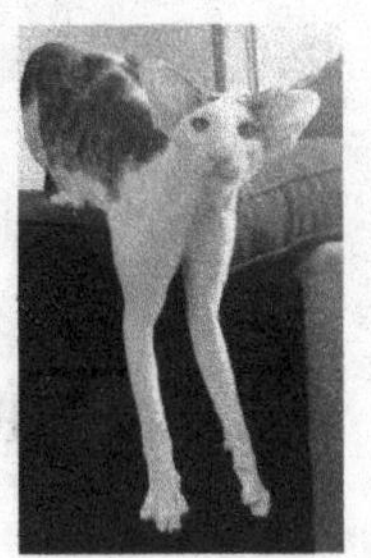

Hello I'm an Oriental short hair

I'm playful and smart

I like children and other pets

I like to talk and need attention to stay sane

I will pick a person and he or she will never go anywhere

without me

The first Oriental shorthair was born in the early 1960s

I will play with whatever I find

Pallas's cat

Hello I'm a Pallas's cat

I like cold rocky places

I can live up to 11.5 years (captive)

I can be up to 9 pounds

I can be up to 25.5 inches long

I'm awake at night

I live in Asia

I eat pika, rodents, insects, and birds

I'm endangered

I'm hunted for my fur

pampas cat

Hello I'm a pampas cat

I live in South America

I can be up to 15 pounds

I can be up to 42 inches long

I can be up to 14 inches tall

I can live up to 16 years (captive)

I'm awake at night

I eat chicken, penguin, and guinea pig

The biggest threat I face is habitat loss

Trading my fur stopped in 1987

Panthera leo fossilis

Hello I'm a lion

I went extinct 340,000 years ago

I could be up to 2.5 meters long

I could be up to 135 centimeters tall

I could be up to 350 kilograms

I lived in the area between Germany and Italy

Panthera leo melanochaita

Hello I'm a lion

I live in Africa

I'm a subspecies that diverged 50,000 years ago

I can be up to 10.8 feet long

I can be up to 600 pounds

Girls hunt in a group

I eat mice, elephants, and whatever I find laying around

I'm protected

I'm hunted because I eat farm animals and because I'm

beautiful

Panthera leo sinhaleyus

Hello I'm a lion

I lived in Shri Lanka

I went extinct in 37,000 BC

In 1939 someone found two of my teeth

Panthera leo vereshchagini

Hello I'm a lion

I went extinct in the Pleistocene

I lived between Alaska and the Yukon

I was smaller than the cave lion

Persian

Hello I'm a Persian

I love adults

I tolerate children and other pets

I like to sit around

Do not broad me in a kennel

I'm prone to bladder, kidney, liver, and retina problems

I may have difficulty breathing

I'm sensitive to heat

I need weekly baths

I need daily brushing, tooth brushing, and eye cleaning

After my bath use a low intensity hair drier to dry me

Persian leopard

Hello I'm a Persian leopard

I live in Iran

I like forests and mountains

I'm endangered

I eat deer and pigs

I'm threatened by habitat loss and poaching

I can be up to 6 feet tall

I can be up to 130 pounds

Peterbald

Hello I'm a Peterbald

I'm from Russia

The first Peterbald was born in 1993

The Peterbald became its own breed in 2005

I'm very intelligent and playful

I love people and try to talk with them

I like to live with other animals

I can have hair or not

Pixie bob

Hello I'm a Pixie bob

I can be up to seventeen pounds

I can be up to twenty-four inches long

I can be up to fifteen years old

I'm very friendly

I love to play

I can have up to seven toes on each foot

The Pixie bob became its own breed in 1995

My teeth and hair need brushed on a regular basis

I like to go for walks

I like water

I'm good with older children

Puma

Hello I'm a Puma

I can live up to twenty years

I can be up to five feet long

I can be up to one hundred fifty-eight pounds

I can jump up to twenty feet

I can live in almost any environment

My home can be up to 125 square miles

I eat deer, pigs, capybaras, racoons, armadillos, hares, and

squirrels

I like to live alone

 I lived with my mom for 18 months

Pumapard

Hello I'm a pumapard

I suffer from dwarfism

The first pumapard was born in Chicago in the 1890s

My parents were a puma and a leopard

The first pumapard belonged to the Ringling brothers

Raas

Hello I'm a Raas

I'm from Indonesia

I'm good luck

According to myth if I'm on a boat with unmarried people

it will sink

According to myth only a cleric can keep me as a pet

I'm energetic and play but I'm shy at first

Keep me indoors or on a leash or I'll leave and never

come back

I need daily tooth brushing

I need brushed twice a week

Start training me as soon as you can

Ragamuffin

Hello I'm a Ragamuffin

I can be up to twelve ponds

I can live up to thirteen years

I need lots of grooming

I like to lay around

I do best with people who play with me a lot

I do best indoors

The first Ragamuffin was born in California

It was the daughter of a ragdoll cat named Josephine

ragdoll

Hello I'm a ragdoll

The first ragdoll was born in California in 1963

I should be kept indoors

I love affection and will follow people around

I like to play fetch and go for walks

I'm prone to bladder stones and hypertrophic

cardiomyopathy

I need daily tooth brushing

I need my nails trimmed every two weeks

I need brushed twice a week

Rhodesian wild cat

Hello I'm a Rhodesian wild cat

I was discovered in 1904

I lived with Neolithic farmers

I have color vision

I can smell meat that is 200 meters away

I like to live alone

I eat rodents and rabbits

Russian blue

Hello I'm a Russian blue

I can be up to twelve ponds

I can be up to twenty years old

I'm shy but loving to my family

I like to play and sleep

I like to talk

I'm very smart

I need my teeth brushed daily

The first Russian blue was born before the 1860s

Russian white

Hello I'm a Russian white

The first Russian white was born in the UK in 1960

I'm quiet

I'm smart and affectionate

I'm playful and I like to learn tricks

I need brushed twice a week

I like puzzles

Rusty spotted cat

Hello I'm a rusty spotted cat

I can be up to 4 pounds

I can be up to 29 inches long

I like forests and grasslands

I live in Shri Lanka and India

I eat rodents, frogs, and domestic birds

The biggest threat to my habitat is deforestation

Sam sawet

Hello I'm a Sam sawet

I'm from Thailand

I can be up to 13 pounds

I can be up to 15 years old

I'm playful and smart

I like kids and other pets

I may have allergies

I'm prone to urinary track disease

I need a weekly brushing

I need a monthly bath

sand cat

Hello I'm a sand cat

I'm almost threatened

I live in the desert

I can be up to 18 inches long

I can be up to eight pounds

I'm awake at night

I eat birds, rodents, snakes, insects, and lizards

I bury my left overs

I like to live alone

I live with my mom for the first 8 months

I can live up to 13 years (captive)

Savannah cat

Hello I'm a Savannah cat

I like water

I love to play and go for walks

I like to follow people and I do well with other animals

I need lots of taurine in my diet

Never give me ketamine

The first Savannah cat was born in April 1986

Scottish fold

Hello I'm a Scottish fold

The first Scottish fold was born in 1961

I'm from Scotland

I'm very quiet

I love people

I like other pets

I should be kept indoors

Scottish straight

Hello I'm a Scottish straight

I'm smart, playful, and friendly

I like children and other pets

I can be up to 15 years old

I can be up to 14 pounds

I can be up to 10 inches tall

The first Scottish straight was born in 1961

I like to be with people

I don't like to be carried

I like to learn tricks

I'm quiet

I need brushed consistently

Selkirk rex

Hello I'm a Selkirk rex

The first Selkirk rex was born in Montana in 1987

We became our own breed in 1994

I'm smart and loving

I even like dogs

I like to learn tricks and solve puzzles

I'm prone to kidney and heart disease

I'm prone to hip problems

I need weekly nail trimming

I need regular tooth brushing

I need my hair brushed multiple times a week

Serengeti cat

Hello I'm a Serengeti cat

I like to talk and play

I like children and other pets

I can be up to ten years old

I can be up to fifteen pounds

I love to climb and jump

I need my nails trimmed weekly

I need my teeth brushed daily

I need occasional brushing

Serrade petit

Hello I'm a serrade petit

I'm from France

I can be up to 9 pounds

I like to play and cuddle

I like children and other pets

I need a weekly brushing

Serval

Hello I'm a serval

I'm from Africa

I like to stay near water

I can live up to 20 years (captive)

I live with my mom for the first 8 months

She makes me leave her territory after the first 2 years

I like to live alone

I eat rodent, fish, insect, bird, frog, and reptile

I'm hunted for my meat and fur

Servical

Hello I'm a Servical

My mom was a caracal

My dad was a serval

We often have organ deformities and poor circulation

Siamese

Hello I'm a Siamese

I like to talk and play

I can be up to 15 years old

I can be up to 20 inches long

I can be up to 14 pounds

I'm from Thailand

In 1878 President Hayes got a Siamese as a gift

I believe that my family needs my constant guidance

I will follow people everywhere

I'm smart

I'm prone to heart defects, asthma, and amyloidosis

Keep me indoors

I need a weekly brushing

Siberian cat

Hello I'm a Siberian cat

I'm from Russia

The first Siberian cat was born 1,000 years ago

I'm loving and friendly

I love to climb

I'm playful

I like to learn tricks

I will follow you around

I'm prone to hypertrophic cardiomyopathy

I need my teeth brushed daily

I need brushed and a nail trimming every week

When I'm molting brush me daily

Siberian tiger

Hello I'm a Siberian tiger

I'm endangered

I can be up to 675 pounds

I can live up to 15 years (wild) 25 years (captive)

I eat deer, moose, boar, bear, hare, rabbit, and salmon

Sinai leopard

Hello I'm a Sinai leopard

I'm from Unguja

I was hunted to extinction because I ate livestock

I was the smallest leopard in the world

I was believed to be a witch's pet

Singapura cat

Hello I'm a Singapura cat

I can live up to fifteen years

I can be up to eight pounds

I'm energetic and playful

I love to explore

I'm prone to pyruvate kinase deficiency

I may need a c section if I'm pregnant

It's not clear if I'm from America or Singapore

The first Singapura was born in the 1970s

Smilodon

Hello I'm a Smilodon

I went extinct 14,000 years ago

My canine teeth were more than ten inches long

I lived in a pack

I ate bears, mammoths, and horses

Snow leopard

Hello I'm a snow leopard

I live in Asia

I'm vulnerable

I can be up to 118 inches long

I can be up to 121 pounds

I eat mountain ungulates

Snowshoe cat

Hello I'm a snowshoe cat

I can be up to 20 years old

I can be up to 12 pounds

I like to climb

I'm friendly and playful

I like children and other pets

I will follow you everywhere

I like to swim

I like to talk

I like to cuddle

The first snowshoe cat was born in the 1960s

Sokoke

Hello I'm a Sokoke

I like to go for walks and learn tricks

I'm loving and intelligent

I like children and other pets

I love to swim and will try to swim in my water dish

I'm from Kenya

I like to climb

Somali cat

Hello I'm a Somali cat

I can be up to 12 pounds

I can be up to 13 years old

I like to talk, jump, and play

I like children and other pets

I like to climb

I need brushed daily

The first Somali was born in the 1960s

Its parents were Abyssinian

South African cheetah

Hello I'm a cheetah

I'm from the Pleistocene

Boys have bigger teeth than girls

I can be up to 84 inches long

I can be up to 35 inches tall

I can be up to 143.3 pounds

I live with my mom for the first 18 months

My favorite food is the oryx

I'm vulnerable

I'm threatened by low genetic diversity, habitat loss, and

poaching

South China tiger

Hello I'm a South China tiger

I'm functionally extinct which means that no South China
tiger lives in the wild

I can be up to 430 pounds

I eat deer, boar, and cattle

I live with my mom for the first 18 months

I like to live and hunt alone

It became illegal to hunt me in 1979

The last wild South China Tiger was born 25 years ago

Southern African wild cat

Hello I'm a southern African

wild cat

I'm from 131000 years ago

I began living with people 10000 years ago

I'm a relative of the domestic cat

Sphynx

Hello I'm a sphynx

I'm from Canada

The first sphynx was born in 1966

I'm loveable, smart, and playful

I like other pets

I need regular baths

I should be kept indoors

Sri Lankan leopard

Hello I'm a Sri Lankan leopard

I'm endangered

I was discovered in 1956

I can be up to 4 feet 8 inches long

I can be up to 220 pounds

I like to live alone

I eat deer, monkey, boar, reptile, and bird

I was once mistaken for a tiger

Sumatran tiger

Hello I'm a Sumatran tiger

I'm critically endangered

I'm from Indonesia

I can be up to 140 kilograms

I'm very shy so I try to avoid people

I've lost a lot of habitat to farming

I'm hunted for my fur

There are only four hundred of us in the wild

I eat pigs and deer

Suphalak

Hello I'm a Suphalak

I'm from Thailand

It is said that I will make my owner rich

I'm intelligent and loving

I need brushed twice a week

I'm very playful

Syrian wild cat

Hello I'm a Syrian wild cat

I'm often confused for a feral domestic cat

Hybridization is possible and common

I'm not considered threatened

I'm awake at night and I like to live alone

I eat rodents and birds

I can live up to 21 years

Tabby

Hello I'm a Tabby

I have the letter M on my forehead

I look like marble

I'm the most common cat

I'm the source of the cat stereo type

Thai cat

Hello I'm a Thai cat

I can be up to 16 years old

I can be up to 15 pounds

I can be up to 23 inches tall

I love attention

I like to cuddle and play

I like children and pets

I do not need brushed often but I like to be groomed

Thai lilac cat

Hello I'm a Thai lilac cat

The first Thai lilac cat was born in 1989

Its mom was a korat

Tigard

Hello I'm a tigard

My mom was a jaguar

My dad was a tiger

I only exist in captivity

At 2 years old I weighed 400 pounds

Tiger

Hello I'm a tiger

I'm from China

I'm from the Pleistocene

I can be up to 12.8 feet long

I can be up to 675 pounds

I like to live alone

I like to swim and bathe

My home can be up to 40.8 miles wide

I might share my food with other tigers

Males might help with the kittens but that is unlikely

Tigon

Hello I'm a tigon

My mom was a lion

My dad was a tiger

I can be up to 400 pounds

Females can have babies but males can not

I only exist in captivity

ti-liger

Hello I'm a ti-liger

My dad was a tiger

My mom was a liger

I can be up to 5.5 meters long

I can be up to 600 kilograms

The first ti-ligers were born in 2013

I only exist in captivity

ti-tigon

Hello I'm a ti-tigon

My dad was a tiger

My mom was a tigon

I only exist in captivity

Tonkinese

Hello I'm a Tonkinese

The first Tonkinese was born in the 1960s

I love to climb and play

I demand attention often

I'm very smart

I like to learn tricks

I need other cats or a dog in my home

I'm prone to periodontal disease

I need weekly brushing and nail trimming

I need daily tooth brushing

Toyger

Hello I'm a Toyger

I'm friendly, smart, and energetic

I like to learn tricks and play

I like children and other pets

The first Toyger was born in America in 1993

I may have heart murmurs

I need weekly nail trimming and brushing

I need daily tooth brushing

Transvaal lion

Hello I'm a Transvaal lion

I eat zebra

I live in Africa

Girls hunt in a group

I can be up to 550 pounds

I can be up to 10 feet long

I can live up to 28 years

I was once hunted for my mane

My pride consists of up to 12 adult females, 3 adult

males, and cubs of both genders

Tristram's wild cat

Hello I'm a Tristram's wild cat

I like to live alone

I can live up to 15 years

I'm awake at night

I eat rodents

Turkestan wild cat

Hello I'm a Turkestan wild cat

I can be up to 8.8 pounds

I do not like high altitudes or deserts

I eat bugs, lizards, and small mammals

I'm hunted for my fur

Turkish angora

Hello I'm a Turkish angora

The first Turkish angora was born

before the 16th century AD

I'm energetic and Playful

I like children and other pets

I will follow people around and demand attention

I like to climb and learn tricks

I'm prone to hypertrophic cardiomyopathy

I may be deaf if I have blue eyes

I might like water

I need a bath every few months

I need daily tooth brushing

I need weekly brushing and nail trimming

Turkish van cat

Hello I'm a Turkish van cat

I'm from Turkey

I'm considered a national treasure

I came to America in 1982

I'm very smart

I love to climb, swim, and play

I like children and other pets

I'm very energetic

I need daily tooth brushing

I need weekly combing and nail trimming

Ugandan wild cat

Hello I'm a Ugandan wild cat

I eat rats, rabbits, mice, insects, birds, eggs, reptiles, and

amphibians

My prey can be as big as I am

I don't like the desert or rainforest

Ukrainian Levkey

Hello I'm a Ukrainian levkey

I can live up to nineteen years

I can weigh up to fifteen pounds

I'm smart

I love to play and talk

The first Ukrainian levkey was born in 2001

I need sun block or a sweater depending on the season

I love other animals and people

The Ukrainian levkey became its own breed in 2005

van cat

Hello I'm a van cat

We were domesticated about 9,000 years ago

I'm friendly

I like to play and swim

I like water

I'm from the Middle East

There are many feral van cats

There is a program in place to stop the recent population

decline

West African lion

Hello I'm a west African lion

I can be up to 10 feet long

My tail can be up to 3 feet long

I can be up to 550 pounds

My home is 100 square miles wide

I eat antelope, zebra, hogs, hippo, buffalo, and wildebeest

I hide my cub for the first six weeks of its life and we

rejoin our pride after that

I'm vulnerable

White panther

Hello I'm a jaguar, leopard, or cougar

I'm either an albino or I have leucism

White lions have leucism

I'm rare in the wild but naturally occurring

I'm not a different species or sub-species

Albinos have red eyes

Individuals with leucism do not

white tiger

Hello I'm a white tiger

I'm inbred

80% of my babies die from birth defects

29 out of every 30 white tiger cubs are put down

I'm not a different subspecies I simply have a mutation

that causes white hair

Only 1 in every 10,000 tigers has the mutation that causes

white fur

The last wild white tiger died in 1958

Wila krungthep

Hello I'm a wila krungthep

I'm from Thailand

The first wila krungthep was born in 2014

And it was discovered on February 6 2018

There are only 40 wila krungtheps on earth

Xenosmilus

Hello I'm a Xenosmilus

I lived one million years ago

I could be up to five hundred pounds

I could be up to five feet long

I eat pigs

I lived in North America

I jumped out of trees and landed on my prey

York chocolate

Hello I'm a York chocolate

I have lots of energy

I'm friendly and playful

I like children and other pets

I can be up to 16 pounds

I can be up to 15 years old

I can be up to 10 inches tall

The first York chocolate was born in 1983

I'm smart

I like water

I love toys that I can chase

Works cited

www.omlet.co.uk/breeds/cats/donskoy_-_don_sphynx_cat

www.hillspet.com/cat-care/cat-breeds/ragamuffin

www.cat-world.com.au/exotic-shorthair-breed-profile.html

en.wikipedia.org/wiki/American_Wirehair

prettylittercats.com/blogs/prettylitter-blog/khao-manee-cats

www.pawculture.com/breed-basics/cat-breeds/savannah-cat-breed/

www.cat-breeds.com/ukrainian-levkoy-cat/

www.thesprucepets.com/pixie-bob-cat-profile-554218

www.tica.org/breeds/browse-all-breeds?view=article&id=865:peterbald-breed&catid=79

www.felineliving.net/lykoi-cat/

www.petguide.com/breeds/cat/minskin/

www.petguide.com/breeds/cat/highlander/

cfa.org/Breeds/BreedsSthruT/Sphynx.aspx

www.vetstreet.com/cats/devon-rex

cfa.org/breeds/breedssthrut/scottishfold.aspx

www.vetstreet.com/cats/norwegian-forest-cat#1_ugw20zmq

www.vetstreet.com/cats/persian#upper-tabs

www.vetstreet.com/cats/egyptian-mau#0_ansjyli2

www.vetstreet.com/cats/cornish-rex

www.vetstreet.com/cats/selkirk-rex#1_wm0slq1w

www.hillspet.com/cat-care/cat-breeds/american-curl

www.hillspet.com/cat-care/cat-breeds/japanese-bobtail

www.vetstreet.com/cats/laperm#upper-tabs

www.purina.com/cats/cat-breeds/manx

www.purina.com/cats/cat-breeds/bombay

www.vetstreet.com/cats/korat#1_ugw20zmq

www.vetstreet.com/cats/balinese

www.vetstreet.com/cats/ragdoll

www.vetstreet.com/cats/maine-coon#1_ugw20zmq

www.google.com/images

www.vetstreet.com/cats/ocicat#1_ugw20zmq

www.vetstreet.com/cats/tonkinese

www.vetstreet.com/cats/turkish-angora#1_ugw20zmq

www.hillspet.com/cat-care/cat-breeds/colorpoint-shorthair

www.purina.com/breeds/bengal-cat

www.vetstreet.com/cats/munchkin

www.hillspet.com/cat-care/cat-breeds/russian-blue

www.vetstreet.com/cats/abyssinian#1_ugw20zmq

www.vetstreet.com/cats/burmese#upper-tabs

www.vetstreet.com/cats/birman#1_ugw20zmq

www.vetstreet.com/cats/british-shorthair#1_ugw20zmq

www.hillspet.com/cat-care/cat-breeds/singapura

www.vetstreet.com/cats/chartreux

www.vetstreet.com/cats/siberian

prettylittercats.com/blogs/prettylitter-blog/sokoke-hybrid-cat-basics

en.wikipedia.org/wiki/Van_cat

www.petguide.com/breeds/cat/serengeti/

www.vetstreet.com/cats/turkish-van

www.petguide.com/breeds/cat/european-burmese/

www.vetstreet.com/cats/burmilla

animals.sandiegozoo.org/animals/mountain-lion-puma-cougar

conservewildcats.org/resources/amur-leopard-facts/

www.thoughtco.com/cave-lion-1093066

www.thoughtco.com/xenosmilus-profile-1093290

www.dkfindout.com/us/dinosaurs-and-prehistoric-life/prehistoric-mammals/smilodon/

www.knowyourcat.info/lib/ashera.htm

messybeast.com/lostbreed-mexican.htm

wildcatconservation.org/wild-cats/eurasia/iberian-lynx/

www.wwfindia.org/about_wwf/priority_species/threatened_species/asiatic_lion/

www.extinctanimals.org/barbary-lion.htm

extinct-animals-facts.com/Extinct-Prehistoric-Animal-Facts/American-Lion-Facts.shtml

bigcatrescue.org/black-panthers/

www.fws.gov/refuge/florida_panther/wah/panther.html

en.wikipedia.org/wiki/Panthera_leo_melanochaita

www.extinctanimals.org/cape-lion.htm

creationwiki.org/Transvaal_lion

wildfact.com/forum/topic-the-congo-lion

www.zsl.org/african-lion-facts

www.livescience.com/27404-lion-facts.html

www.thoughtco.com/european-lion-1093081

prehistoric-fauna.com/Panthera-leo-fossilis

en.wikipedia.org/wiki/Panthera_leo_sinhaleyus

www.facebook.com/PrehistoricFauna/photos/panthera-leo-vereshchagini-also-known-as-the-east-siberian-or-beringian-cave-lio/347672935341408/

www.fauna-flora.org/species/sumatran-tiger

www.thoughtco.com/caspian-tiger-1093063

extinct-animals-facts.com/Recently-Extinct-Animal-Facts/Bali-Tiger-Facts.shtml

onekindplanet.org/animal/tiger-south-china/

www.tigers-world.com/malayan-tiger/

animalstime.com/javan-tiger-facts/

www.tigers-world.com/indochinese-tiger/

www.softschools.com/facts/animals/sand_cat_facts/529/

bigcatrescue.org/flat-headed-cat-facts/

bigcatrescue.org/rusty-spotted-cat-facts/

bigcatrescue.org/black-footed-cat-facts/

bigcatrescue.org/margay-facts/

www.panthera.org/cat/snow-leopard

www.fresnochaffeezoo.org/species/african-lion/

en.wikipedia.org/wiki/Tiger

bigcatrescue.org/clouded-leopard-facts

www.awf.org/wildlife-conservation/leopard

www.lynxuk.org/lynx.html

www.visionsoftheworld.org/tigers

en.wikipedia.org/wiki/Siberian_tiger

onekindplanet.org/animal/bengal-tiger/

www.wildcatsanctuary.org/8-fast-facts-white-tigers/

bigcatrescue.org/jungle-cat-facts

animalfactguide.com/animal-facts/cougar/

bigcatrescue.org/ocelot-facts

www.softschools.com/facts/animals/marbled_cat_facts/632/

bigcatrescue.org/iriomote-cat-facts

www.theanimalfiles.com/mammals/carnivores/cheetah.html

bigcatrescue.org/leopard-cat-facts

www.softschools.com/facts/animals/oncilla_facts/309/

bigcatrescue.org/chinese-mountain-cat-facts

bigcatrescue.org/bobcat-facts

bigcatrescue.org/bay-cat-facts

www.softschools.com/facts/animals/kodkod_facts/1112/

www.wildcatfamily.com/puma-lineage/cheetah-acinonyx-jubatus/

www.wikiwand.com/en/Southeast_African_cheetah

dinoanimals.com/animals/cheetah-the-fastest-land-animal-in-the-world/

animalsadda.com/aegean-cat-facts-price-pictures-breeders-puppies/

www.softschools.com/facts/animals/african_golden_cat_facts/687/

study.com/academy/lesson/african-leopard-facts-lesson-for-kids.html

uganda365.com/african-leopard-facts/

en.wikipedia.org/wiki/Wildcat

bigcatrescue.org/anatolian-leopards/

bigcatrescue.org/andean-mountain-cat-facts

www.petguide.com/breeds/cat/aphrodite-giant/

saudi-archaeology.com/subjects/arabian-leopard/

www.petguide.com/breeds/cat/arabian-mau/

bigcatrescue.org/wildcat-facts/

bigcatrescue.org/pallas-cat-facts/

bigcatrescue.org/pampas-cat-facts/

perfectpersianleopard.weebly.com/basic-facts.html

en.wikipedia.org/wiki/Pumapard

animalsadda.com/australian-mist/

animalsadda.com/asian-semi-longhair-facts-pictures-kitten-price/

en.wikipedia.org/wiki/Asiatic_cheetah

www.softschools.com/facts/animals/wildcat_facts/1324/

www.petguide.com/breeds/cat/bambino/

bigcatrescue.org/caracal-facts

www.petguide.com/breeds/cat/ojos-azules-cat/

en.wikipedia.org/wiki/Liger

www.macroevolution.net/leopon.html

en.wikipedia.org/wiki/Panthera_hybrid#Lipard

en.wikipedia.org/wiki/Congolese_spotted_lion

en.wikipedia.org/wiki/Litigon

en.wikipedia.org/wiki/Liliger

en.wikipedia.org/wiki/Tigon

en.wikipedia.org/wiki/Panthera_hybrid#Jaguar_and_tiger_hybrids

en.wikipedia.org/wiki/Tiliger

listserv.linguistlist.org/pipermail/ads-l/2005-May/050174.html

www.viovet.co.uk/breed_information/1-17/Brazilian-Shorthair

www.petguide.com/breeds/cat/british-longhair/

www.europetnet.org/pet-resources/cat-breeds/item/1911-british-semi-longhair.html

blog.rhinoafrica.com/2011/08/19/five-lesser-known-wild-cats-africa/

www.petguide.com/breeds/cat/york-chocolate/

en.wikipedia.org/wiki/Wildcat

www.sa-venues.com/wildlife/african-wild-cat.htm

file:///C:/Users/TEMP/AppData/Local/Microsoft/Windows/INetCache/IE/8NFM5GOR/002__057__publications__policies__Scottish_wildcat_policy___October_2011__1320168159.pdf

www.petguide.com/breeds/cat/california-spangled/

bigcatrescue.org/canada-lynx-facts/

en.wikipedia.org/wiki/Caraval

en.wikipedia.org/wiki/White_panther#White_panther_types

pet-az.com/en/fun-i-social/pet-news/wila-krungthep-cat.html

www.petguide.com/breeds/cat/cashmere-cat/

en.wikipedia.org/wiki/Caucasian_wildcat

www.hillspet.com/cat-care/cat-breeds/chantilly

www.petguide.com/breeds/cat/chausie/

bigcatrescue.org/cheetah-facts/

www.petguide.com/breeds/cat/cheetoh/

www.softschools.com/facts/animals/lynx_facts/329/

bigcatrescue.org/fishing-cat-facts/

www.petguide.com/breeds/cat/foldex/

en.wikipedia.org/wiki/Panthera_hybrid#Jaguar_and_leopard_hybrids

en.wikipedia.org/wiki/Panthera_hybrid#Jagupard

en.wikipedia.org/wiki/Panthera_hybrid#Jaguar_and_lion_hybrids

en.wikipedia.org/wiki/Corsican_wildcat

www.vetstreet.com/cats/cymric

www.viovet.co.uk/breed_information/1-31/Cyprus-Shorthair

www.petguide.com/breeds/cat/domestic-medium-hair/

www.hillspet.com/cat-care/cat-breeds/domestic-shorthair

www.viovet.co.uk/breed_information/1-35/Dragon-Li

www.petguide.com/breeds/cat/dwelf/

thepetwiki.com/wiki/elf_cat/

www.hillspet.com/cat-care/cat-breeds/european-shorthair

bigcatrescue.org/geoffroy-cat-facts/

www.hillspet.com/cat-care/cat-breeds/german-rex

tenikwa.com/african-wild-cat-fact-sheet/

www.vetstreet.com/cats/havana-brown#0_b9i3ci6z

www.softschools.com/facts/cats/himalayan_cat_facts/2631/

en.wikipedia.org/wiki/Indian_leopard

en.wikipedia.org/wiki/Indochinese_leopard

animalia.bio/wildcat

messybeast.com/genetics/hyb-jagxleop.htm

en.wikipedia.org/wiki/Panthera_hybrid#Jaguar_and_lion_hybrids

www.panthera.org/cat/jaguar

bigcatrescue.org/jaguarundi-facts

en.wikipedia.org/wiki/Javan_leopard

www.hillspet.com/cat-care/cat-breeds/javanese

en.wikipedia.org/wiki/Southern_African_wildcat

1zootree.weebly.com/korean-bobtail.html

catbreedsinformation.blogspot.com/2015/06/korn-ja-cat.html

www.dogalize.com/2017/03/cat-breeds-korn-ja-cat-personality/

www.vetstreet.com/cats/kurilian-bobtail

en.wikipedia.org/wiki/Asian_cat#Origin

www.petguide.com/breeds/cat/mekong-bobtail/

www.catster.com/lifestyle/in-the-wild-cats-fascinating-facts-about-the-pallas-cat

www.petguide.com/breeds/cat/napoleon-cat/

cattime.com/cat-breeds/nebelung-cats

allanimalia.com/103/north-chinese-leopard-facts.html

kidsanimalsfacts.com/northwest-african-cheetah-facts-for-kids/

www.viovet.co.uk/breed_information/1-57/Oregon-Rex

www.petguide.com/breeds/cat/oriental-bicolor/

www.thesprucepets.com/oriental-longhair-cat-breed-profile-4769416

www.petfinder.com/cat-breeds/oriental/

www.catbreedselector.com/raas-cat.asp

mammalia.fandom.com/wiki/Wildcat

www.dogalize.com/2017/04/cat-breeds-russian-white-black-tabby/

www.catbreedselector.com/sam-sawet-cat.asp

www.petguide.com/breeds/cat/scottish-straight/

www.dogalize.com/2017/04/cat-breeds-serrade-petit-cat-characteristics-behavior/

bigcatrescue.org/serval-facts/

bigcatrescue.org/jojo/

cattime.com/cat-breeds/siamese-cats

www.interestingworldfacts.com/10-interesting-facts-about-zanzibar-leopard/

www.hillspet.com/cat-care/cat-breeds/snowshoe

www.hillspet.com/cat-care/cat-breeds/somali

www.catsforafrica.co.za/african-wildcat-felis-lybica/

en.wikipedia.org/wiki/Sri_Lankan_leopard

www.dogalize.com/2017/04/cat-breeds-suphalak-cat-chatacteristics-behavior/

en.wikipedia.org/wiki/Wildcat

en.wikipedia.org/wiki/Asiatic_wildcat

www.vetstreet.com/cats/toyger

www.dogalize.com/2017/04/cat-breeds-thai-lilac-cat-characteristics-behavior/

en.wikipedia.org/wiki/Tabby_cat

www.petguide.com/breeds/cat/thai-cat/

www.ingramcontent.com/pod-product-compliance
Lightning Source LLC
Chambersburg PA
CBHW012253240726

48655CB00009B/3288